DISCOVERING Space

THE NEAR PLANETS

Ian Graham

Smart Apple Media

Published by Smart Apple Media
2140 Howard Drive West
North Mankato, MN 56003
Created by Q2A Media

Series Editor: Honor Head
Designers: Diksha Khatri, Ashita Murgai
Picture Researchers: Lalit Dalal, Jyoti Sachdev

Picture credits
t=top b=bottom c=center l=left r=right m=middle
Cover images: Nasa: t, ml, mr, Science Photo Library/ Photolibrary: b
Small images: Science Photo Library/ Photolibrary: ml, Calvin J. Hamilton: cml, Nasa: cmr, mr.
Nasa/ JPL-Caltech: 4t, 5t, 19t, Science Photo Library/ Photolibrary: 4b, 6b, 7t, 9t, 9b, 11b, 12 (background),
16b, 17 (background), 20b, 21t, 27m, Nasa: 5b, 12b, 14t, 15b, 21b, 25t, 26-27 (background), 26b,
Jurgen Ziewe/ Shutterstock: 7b, Nasa Copyright Free Policy: 8b, 22m, ESA - AOES Medialab: 10-11 (background),
Calvin J. Hamilton: 10b, Corbis: 13t, Earth Observatory/ Nasa: 14-15 (background), Pacific Stock/ Photolibrary:
17b, U.S. Space & Rocket Center: 18-19 (background), JPL/ Nasa: 18b, Peter Arnold Images Inc/ Photolibrary:
23b, ESA: 24 (background), 24b.

Printed in China

Library of Congress Cataloging-in-Publication Data

Graham, Ian, 1953-
The near planets / by Ian Graham.
p. cm. – (Discovering space)
Includes index.
ISBN 978-1-59920-071-2
1. Inner planets—Juvenile literature. I. Title

QB606.G73 2007
523.4—dc22   2007004876

First Edition

9 8 7 6 5 4 3 2 1

Contents

The near planets

Some **planets** are small and rocky, and others are giant gas planets. The four planets closest to the sun belong to the group of small rocky planets. They are Mercury, Venus, Earth, and Mars.

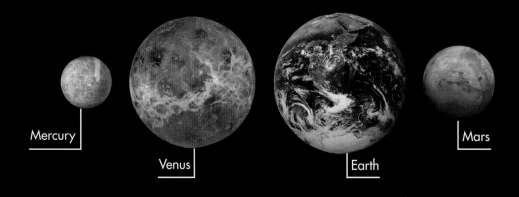

Mercury

Venus

Earth

Mars

Hot rocks

These four planets are called the near planets. They formed at the same time as the sun. They were so hot to begin with that they melted. Over millions of years, the heat slowly escaped into space. As each planet cooled down, its surface hardened to a rocky **crust**.

Meteorites crashed into the young Earth when it was forming.

Surrounded by gas

Most of the near planets are surrounded by a mixture of gases called an **atmosphere**. A planet's **gravity** holds the atmosphere in place around the planet. The bigger the planet, the stronger its gravity. Venus and Earth are the biggest of the near planets. They have the strongest gravity and the thickest atmospheres. Mars is smaller, so it has a very thin atmosphere. Mercury is the smallest of the near planets. Its gravity is too weak to hold on to an atmosphere so it has almost none.

White clouds of water droplets swirl around Earth's atmosphere.

The Earth's moon is the biggest **moon** orbiting any of the four near planets.

Spotlight on
space

The eight planets of the solar system have more than 150 moons, but only three of these moons orbit the four near planets. Mercury and Venus have no moons. Earth has one big moon. Mars has two tiny moons.

Mercury

Mercury is the smallest of the near planets and is the planet closest to the sun. It is not much bigger than the Earth's moon, and if it could be seen up close, it would look like the moon, too.

Hot and cold

Mercury is so close to the sun that the side facing the sun is heated to 752 °F (400 °C). That is four times as hot as boiling water. The side facing away from the sun plunges to –328 °F (–200 °C), which is way below freezing.

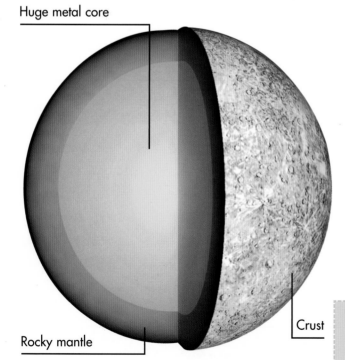

Huge metal core

Rocky mantle

Crust

Mercury facts

Size across the middle	3,031 miles (4,878 km)
Distance from the sun	36 million miles (58 million km)
Gravity	about one-third the strength of Earth's gravity
Atmosphere	none
Moons	none
Length of day	176 Earth days
Length of year	88 Earth days

For such a small planet, Mercury has a huge metal **core**.

The largest feature on the surface of Mercury is a vast crater called the Caloris Basin. It was made when a giant rock hit Mercury. The crater is 839 miles (1,350 km) across. That makes it one of the biggest craters anywhere in the solar system. A crater this big is also called an impact basin. When the rock hit Mercury, the ground on the other side of the planet bent and cracked. Scientists call it the Weird Terrain.

Mercury is covered with craters caused by rocks from space crashing into it.

Spotlight on
space

Although Mercury travels around the sun very quickly, it spins slowly. This means that a day on Mercury is twice as long as a year on Mercury.

Mercury

Sun

Mercury travels around the sun four times faster than Earth does.

Exploring Mercury

Mercury is a difficult planet to explore because it is so close to the sun. A **space probe** visiting Mercury has to be able to survive the sun's scorching heat. Mercury has been visited by only one space probe so far, but another is on the way.

Mariner 10

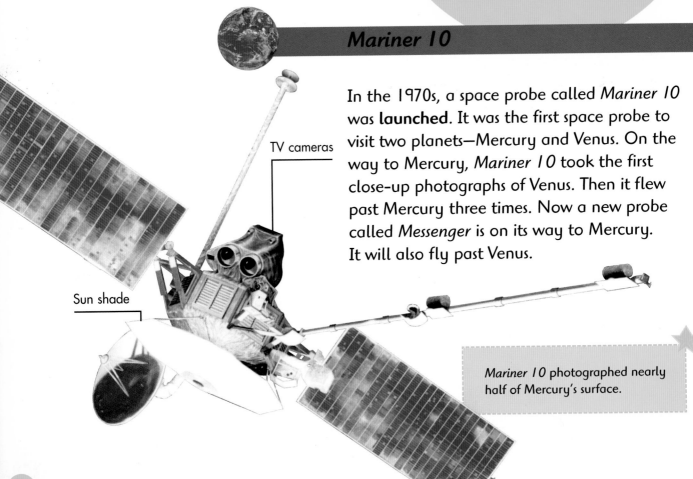

TV cameras

Sun shade

In the 1970s, a space probe called *Mariner 10* was **launched**. It was the first space probe to visit two planets—Mercury and Venus. On the way to Mercury, *Mariner 10* took the first close-up photographs of Venus. Then it flew past Mercury three times. Now a new probe called *Messenger* is on its way to Mercury. It will also fly past Venus.

Mariner 10 photographed nearly half of Mercury's surface.

This picture was taken by *Mariner 10* during the three flybys in 1974-75.

BepiColombo

A new space mission to Mercury called *BepiColombo* will begin in the year 2013. It is named after the space scientist Giuseppe (Bepi) Colombo. He was the scientist who suggested sending the *Mariner 10* space probe past Venus on its way to Mercury. Two *BepiColombo* space probes will be launched to study Mercury in more detail.

The *Messenger* space probe will spend a year in orbit around Mercury.

Messenger mission

Launched	▶	August 3, 2004
Earth flyby	▶	August 2, 2005
First Venus flyby	▶	October 24, 2006
Second Venus flyby	▶	June 6, 2007
First Mercury flyby	▶	January 15, 2008
Second Mercury flyby	▶	October 6, 2008
Third Mercury flyby	▶	September 30, 2009

Venus

Venus is the second planet from the sun and the closest to Earth. It is about the same size as Earth, but it is a very different planet. If humans stood on its surface, they would be roasted, crushed, and poisoned, all at the same time.

Hothouse planet

The surface of Venus is always hidden under the planet's thick atmosphere. Because much of the sun's heat is trapped by the atmosphere, the temperature soars to 896 °F (480 °C). That is hotter than Mercury. The atmosphere is so thick that it presses down nearly 100 times more than Earth's atmosphere. This would immediately crush a human being.

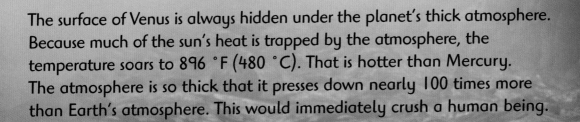

Venus facts

Size across the middle	▶	7,521 miles (12,104 km)
Distance from the sun	▶	67 million miles (108 million km)
Gravity	▶	nearly the same strength as Earth's gravity
Atmosphere	▶	mostly carbon dioxide
Moons	▶	none
Length of day	▶	117 Earth days
Length of year	▶	225 Earth days

The clouds on Venus contain **sulfuric acid**, which burns and chokes.

Wrong spin

Venus spins more slowly than any other planet, and it spins in the opposite direction. On Earth, the sun rises in the east every morning; on Venus, the sun rises in the west. Venus spins so slowly that there are less than two Venus days in a Venus year. When the planets formed, they were all spinning in the same direction, and no one knows why Venus changed direction. Some scientists think it might have been hit by a giant space rock that caused it to start spinning in the opposite direction.

A volcano erupting on Venus's surface might look like this.

The *Venera 9* lander could stay on the surface of Venus for only two hours because of the atmosphere and heat.

Spotlight on
space

Scientists got their first view of the surface of Venus in 1975. The Russian space probe *Venera 9* sent a lander craft down to the surface. It took one picture. This showed flat slabs of rocks scattered all over the surface.

Mapping Venus

To find out more about Venus, scientists had to design and build a **spacecraft** that could see through the thick clouds around the planet and make maps of its surface. The result was the *Pioneer Venus*, which was sent to Venus in 1978.

Seeing the surface

Part of its mission was to make maps of the surface of the planet, while cameras and instruments on board recorded other information. In 1989, a bigger and better spacecraft called *Magellan* was sent to Venus.

Colors have been added to this map of Venus. Yellow shows the highest ground; blue shows the lowest.

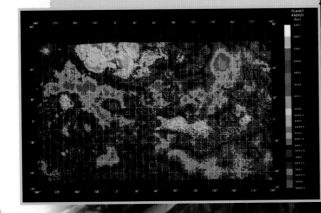

The *Magellan* spacecraft was launched by a **space shuttle**.

The two spacecraft, *Pioneer Venus* and *Magellan*, sent radio waves through Venus's thick clouds. The radio waves bounced off the planet, and the spacecraft used the reflected waves to figure out the shape of the surface.

The *Magellan* space probe spent four years orbiting Venus and mapping its surface. The information was beamed to Earth by radio.

Under the clouds

Magellan mission

Launched	▶	May 5, 1989
Arrived at Venus	▶	August 10, 1990
Mapping began	▶	September 15, 1990
Spacecraft destroyed	▶	October 13, 1994

Scientists thought Venus might look like Earth but without water or life. However, the probes revealed that Venus has a large number of volcanoes. There are also not as many craters as scientists had expected. Scientists think **lava** from Venus's many volcanoes must have flooded the planet's surface and covered up most of the craters. The *Magellan* space probe eventually entered Venus's atmosphere and was destroyed.

Earth—our home planet

Earth is the third planet from the sun and the biggest of the four near planets. It is the only planet known to have life. Earth has one moon, simply called the "moon," that can be seen in the night sky.

Nearly three-quarters of Earth's surface is covered with water.

Earth facts

Size across the middle	▶	7926 miles (12,756 km)
Distance from the Sun	▶	93 million miles (150 million km)
Gravity	▶	one-G
Atmosphere	▶	mainly nitrogen and oxygen
Moons	▶	1
Length of day	▶	24 hours
Length of year	▶	365.25 days

Water world

Earth is like a colorful ball floating in black space. Its surface is covered by blue oceans, green and brown land, and white **ice caps**. It is the only planet with oceans and seas. Water and heat from the sun made it possible for life to develop on Earth.

Earth's seasons

Earth tilts like a spinning top that leans over. When the top half of Earth tilts toward the sun, it is summer in northern Europe and North America. When it is summer in the north, it is winter in the south. As Earth moves along its orbit to the other side of the sun, it tilts away from the sun. The land and the air cool down and the season changes from summer to fall and then to winter.

Earth is a planet of vast oceans and islands, clouds and rain, and volcanoes and mountains.

The same side of the moon always faces Earth.

Spotlight on
space

Of all the moons orbiting the planets, only four other moons are bigger than Earth's. Three of these belong to Jupiter and are called Io, Ganymede, and Callisto. The fourth moon belongs to Saturn and is called Titan.

From core to crust

Earth is not the same all the way through. When it formed, the heaviest materials sank to the center and became Earth's core. Lighter materials floated on top of the core.

Metal and rock

Earth's core is made of metal, mainly iron. The center is solid, but the outer part of the core is liquid metal. The core is surrounded by a hot, slowly flowing rock called the mantle. This is covered by a thin crust of solid rock. We live on top of the crust.

The center of Earth is as hot as the surface of the sun.

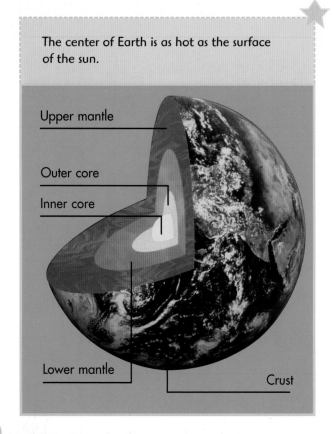

Upper mantle

Outer core

Inner core

Lower mantle

Crust

Inside Earth

Inner core	►	1,727 miles (2,780 km) across
Outer core	►	about 1,274 miles (2,050 km) thick
Mantle	►	about 1,796 miles (2,890 km) thick
Crust	►	about 31 miles (50 km) thick

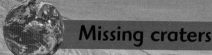

Missing craters

Earth is close to the moon, so it must have been hit by as many space rocks as the moon. But the moon is covered with thousands of craters, and Earth has very few. The weather, water, earthquakes, and volcanoes have changed Earth's surface, so most of the craters on Earth have slowly disappeared.

Spotlight on
space

Earth's crust is like a cracked eggshell. It is made of slowly moving plates of rock. Some of these plates push into each other, some rub against each other, and others pull apart. This can cause earthquakes and volcanoes.

The San Andreas Fault in California is a long crack in the ground where two **plates** of Earth's crust meet.

Volcanoes force hot rock from inside Earth to break through Earth's crust.

Mars—the red planet

Mars is known as the red planet because it is covered with rust-red dust. In many ways, it is like Earth. It has ice caps at its north and south **poles,** and it tilts, so it has seasons like Earth.

Looking for water

On March 10, 2006, a space probe called *Mars Reconnaissance Orbiter* was sent into orbit around Mars. The probe is sending back the clearest pictures of Mars ever taken, and it is looking for signs of water. It joined three other spacecraft in orbit around Mars—*Mars Global Surveyor, Mars Odyssey,* and *Mars Express.*

Mars facts

Size across the middle	4,217 miles (6,786 km)
Distance from the Sun	141.5 million miles (228 million km)
Gravity	about one-third of the strength of Earth's gravity
Atmosphere	mainly carbon dioxide
Moons	2
Length of day	about 40 minutes longer than an Earth day
Length of year	687 Earth days

From space, the *Mars Reconnaissance Orbiter's* cameras can see rocks as small as 8 inches (20 cm) across on the surface of Mars.

Spotlight on
space

The biggest volcano in the solar system is on Mars. It is called Olympus Mons. It is 15 miles (24 km) high, nearly three times the height of Mount Everest, the tallest mountain on Earth.

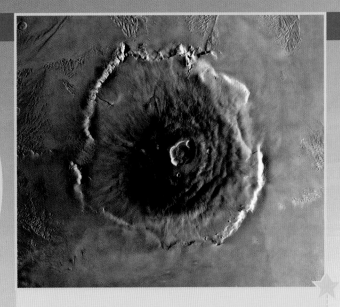

Olympus Mons is a giant volcano on Mars. It could be as much as 200 million years old.

Moons

Mars has two small moons called Phobos and Deimos. Phobos is the larger moon, but its diameter is only 17 miles (27 km). It orbits 3,728 miles (6,000 km) above Mars, so it is about 60 times closer to Mars than the moon is to Earth. Phobos is slowly moving even closer to Mars, and in 50 million years, it will crash into the surface. The other moon, Deimos, has a diameter of only 9.3 miles (15 km). Both moons may be space rocks that were trapped by Mars's gravity.

This crater on Mars is called Endurance. It was formed by a rock from space that crashed into the planet.

Life on Mars

More than one hundred years ago, some **astronomers** thought they could see lines on the surface of Mars. They wondered if these lines might be canals built by **Martians** to move water around the planet.

Visiting Mars

The *Mariner 4* space probe flew past Mars in 1965. It took the first close-up photographs of the planet. There were no canals and no Martian cities in the pictures. Today, scientists believe the lines were an optical illusion, possibly created by drifting dust on Mars.

The two *Viking* spacecraft that landed on Mars took spectacular photographs of the planet's surface.

Spotlight on
space

In 1976, two spacecraft called *Viking 1* and *Viking 2* landed on Mars to study the weather. They also collected some soil and tested it for signs of life, but the tests found no life.

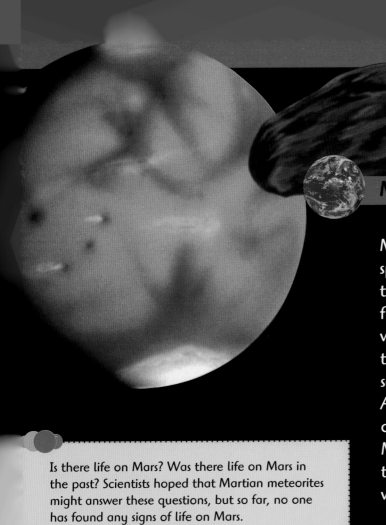

Mars worms?

Mars has been hit by big rocks from space many times in the past. When they landed, they sent many rocks flying, and some of these flew all the way into space. Amazingly, a few of these rocks landed on Earth. In 1996, scientists examined a Mars rock called ALH84001. They found tiny worm-like objects that might have been alive on Mars in the past. Other scientists think this is not possible and are still not sure what these objects are.

Is there life on Mars? Was there life on Mars in the past? Scientists hoped that Martian meteorites might answer these questions, but so far, no one has found any signs of life on Mars.

Some thought the first maps of Mars showed canals crisscrossing the planet, but scientists later found that they did not exist.

Viking missions

Viking 1 launched	▶	August 20, 1975
Viking 2 launched	▶	September 9, 1975
Viking 1 landed on Mars	▶	July 20, 1976
Viking 2 landed on Mars	▶	September 3, 1976

Robot explorers

By 2006, about 12 spacecraft had either crashed into Mars or landed safely. Three of the spacecraft were **rover vehicles** that moved across the surface of Mars to study the rocks and soil. They took thousands of photographs and sent weather reports back to Earth.

Mars rovers

At the beginning of 2004, two Mars exploration rovers landed safely on opposite sides of the planet. One was called *Spirit* and the other was called *Opportunity*. Scientists on Earth moved them by remote control and sent them out to explore the planet's surface and collect information.

A Mars exploration rover drives across the rocky Martian surface.

Mars exploration rover mission

		Spirit	Opportunity
Launched	▶	June 10, 2003	July 7, 2003
Landed on Mars	▶	January 4, 2004	January 25, 2004
Landing site	▶	Gusev crater	Meridiani terra

A day on Mars

Every day, *Spirit* and *Opportunity* are given instructions by scientists on Earth. When one of the rovers reaches an interesting rock, its arm stretches out to scrape away the surface and reveal the rock underneath. It then sends photographs and other information back to Earth, where the next day's work is planned. Each rover was expected to last for about three months, but both were still working more than two years later.

The surface of Mars is covered with red rocks and dust. Strong winds sometimes create dust storms.

Manned missions

Only robots have landed on Mars so far, but there are now plans to send astronauts to the red planet. Before the end of the 21st century, people could be walking on Mars for the first time. Mars will be the first planet to be visited by astronauts.

A Mars base may be built near the South Pole.

This is an artist's impression of what spacecraft to Mars might look like.

Aurora—the first mission

The European Space Agency has a plan called *Aurora* to send astronauts to the moon and then to Mars. At first, they only plan to send robots. If this stage is successful, the ESA will decide if they want to send astronauts.

Going to Mars

There are several other plans for sending people to Mars. One of these plans begins by sending an unmanned spacecraft to Mars, ahead of the astronauts, with enough fuel to bring the astronauts home at the end of the mission. Or an empty spacecraft might land on Mars and make enough fuel for the trip home from gas in the Martian atmosphere. Scientists need to be sure they have a way of getting the astronauts back to Earth before they send them to Mars. The astronauts would spend 18 months exploring Mars.

Astronauts will need spacesuits on Mars because there is not enough **oxygen** in the atmosphere to breathe.

Spotlight on
space

Before astronauts go to Mars, everything they use will be tested in "Mars" bases built on Earth. These bases will copy the way life would be on Mars. Any problems can then be corrected before the Mars missions take place.

Aurora time line

2011	▶	A rover called *Exo-Mars* will be sent to Mars.
2014	▶	Equipment and spacecraft will be tested for a manned landing on Mars.
2016	▶	An unmanned mission will be sent to bring Mars rocks back to Earth.
2018	▶	Engines and landing systems will be tested for a manned mission to Mars.
2024	▶	A manned mission will go to the moon.
2026	▶	An unmanned test-flight will be sent to Mars.
2030–33	▶	The first manned mission to Mars will take place.

Living on Mars

The first manned space missions to Mars will land astronauts on the planet for a few months and then bring them back to Earth. But one day, the red planet could become a second home for humans.

Spotlight on space

Dangerous radiation from space travels through the Martian atmosphere all the way to the ground. One way people might protect themselves from radiation is by living under the surface of the planet.

Changing Mars

Some scientists think Mars can be changed to make it more like Earth. A thicker atmosphere would stop some of the harmful **radiation** from reaching the ground. It would also soak up more of the sun's energy and increase the temperature on Mars. Oxygen would have to be added for people to breathe. If this could be done, people would be able to live on Mars without wearing spacesuits.

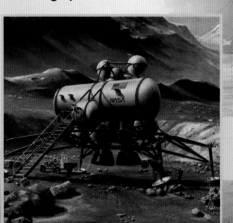

The first buildings on Mars will be built by connecting parts from rockets and spacecraft.

Living off the planet

Making a planet more like Earth is called **terraforming**. The first people to live on Mars will have to bring everything they need with them from Earth. But if terraforming is successful, humans will eventually be able to make all they need on Mars. They will be able to make bricks for building from the Martian soil, they will produce oxygen to breathe from the Martian atmosphere, and they will grow vegetables and plants under huge domes.

Living on Mars

- ▶ Mars is colder than Earth.
- ▶ Gravity is weaker than on Earth.
- ▶ The seasons are twice as long as on Earth.
- ▶ The days are about the same length as on Earth.

One day, people might live inside domes on Mars. The domes will hold air in and keep radiation out.

Making Mars a suitable place for humans to live will take many years.

Time line

3000 B.C.
The Babylonians describe Mercury in their writings.

240 B.C.
The Greek astronomer and poet Eratosthenes measures the size of Earth.

A.D. 1609
The English mathematician Thomas Harriott draws the first map of the moon with the help of a telescope.

1639
Venus is seen crossing in front of the sun.

1659
Markings are seen on the surface of Mars for the first time.

1666
Polar ice caps are seen on Mars for the first time.

1761
Venus's atmosphere is discovered.

1877
The Italian astronomer Giovanni Schiaparelli sees lines on Mars and calls them "canali," meaning canals.

1959
The Russian space probe *Luna 1* is the first to fly past the moon.

Luna 2 is the first probe to crash into the moon.

Luna 3 is the first probe to photograph the far side of the moon.

1962
Mariner 2 flies past Venus.

1965
Mariner 4 takes close-up photographs of Mars.

1966
The Russian space probe, *Luna 9*, makes the first controlled landing on the moon.

The U.S. space probe *Surveyor 1* lands on the moon.

1969
Apollo 11 makes the first manned landing on the moon.

1970
The Russian space probe *Venera 7* makes the first controlled landing on Venus.

1971
U.S. space probe *Mariner 9* goes into orbit around Mars.

1972
Apollo 17 makes the last manned landing on the moon in the 20th century.

1973
Mariner 10 is launched on a mission to Mercury.

1974
Mariner 10 flies past Venus in February and flies past Mercury in March and again in September.

1975
Venera 9 and *Venera 10* land on Venus and send back the first pictures taken from its surface.

1975
Mariner 10 flies past Mercury for the third and last time.

1976
Viking 1 and *Viking 2* land on Mars.

1978
The *Pioneer* space probe is launched on a mission to Venus.

1989
The *Magellan* space probe is launched to make detailed maps of Venus.

1991
Galileo flies past Venus on its way to Jupiter.

1996
The *Lunar Prospector* space probe detects water on the moon.

The *Mars Pathfinder* mission is launched to Mars.

1997
Mars Pathfinder lands on Mars and unloads a small robot rover called *Sojourner* to explore the surface.

Mars Global Surveyor goes into orbit around Mars.

1998
Cassini flies past Venus on its way to Saturn.

The *Mars Climate Orbiter* space probe is launched.

1999
The *Mars Climate Orbiter* is destroyed when it flies too close to Mars.

2001
Mars Odyssey goes into orbit around Mars.

2002
Mars Odyssey begins mapping the surface of Mars and searching for water.

2003
The British Mars lander *Beagle 2* arrives at Mars, but no radio signal is received from it.

The Mars exploration rovers *Spirit* and *Opportunity* are launched.

2004
The Mars exploration rovers *Spirit* and *Opportunity* land on Mars.

The *Messenger* space probe is launched on its way to Mercury.

2005
The U.S. space probe *Mars Reconnaissance Orbiter* is launched.

The European space probe *Venus Express* is launched.

2006
Mars Reconnaissance Orbiter goes into orbit around Mars.

Venus Express goes into orbit around Venus.

2007
The *Phoenix* Mars lander is due to be launched to Mars.

2011
The *Messenger* space probe is due to go into orbit around Mercury.

2013
The two space probes of the *BepiColombo* space mission are due to be launched to Mercury.

2019
BepiColombo is due to arrive at Mercury.

Glossary

astronomers Scientists who study astronomy—the stars, moons, and planets.

atmosphere The gas around a planet or moon. Earth's atmosphere is made of air.

core A planet's core is its center. The four near planets have cores made of metal, mainly iron.

crater A shallow circular dip in the surface of a planet or moon caused by a space rock smashing into it.

crust The rocky surface layer of a planet or a satellite like the moon.

gravity An invisible force that pulls things toward each other. Earth's gravity pulls us down onto the ground and keeps the moon in orbit around Earth.

ice caps Frozen water covering the poles of a planet.

impact basin A huge crater, more than 186 miles (300 km) across, caused by a giant rock hitting a planet or moon.

lander craft A spacecraft designed to land on other planets.

launched When a spacecraft takes off at the beginning of its spaceflight.

lava The hot liquid rock that pours out of a volcano.

mantle A layer of rock below Earth's crust and above the core.

Martians Beings from Mars. It has been proven that there are no living beings on Mars.

meteorites Rocks that fall onto a planet from space.

moon A small object orbiting a planet. Earth has one moon, called the "moon."

one-G The force of gravity on the surface of Earth.

orbit To move around the sun as a planet does, or to move around a planet as a satellite, such as the moon, moves around Earth.

oxygen A gas in the air that is needed for survival by most of the life on Earth.

planets Very big objects in space that orbit a star.

plates Large pieces of rock that make up Earth's crust, which constantly move very slowly. Sometimes plates bump into each other, causing an earthquake.

poles Two points at the farthest north and south of a planet.

radiation Particles or waves given off by something. Solar radiation is made of the particles and waves given off by the sun.

radio waves Energy waves, similar to light waves, but the waves are longer.

reconnaissance Closely watching or studying something to collect information. The *Mars Reconnaissance Orbiter* is a space probe designed to closely watch Mars.

rover vehicles Robot or radio-controlled vehicles that move around the surface of a planet.

solar system The sun, planets, moons, and everything else that orbit the sun.

spacecraft A machine sent into space. Manned spacecraft have people inside. Unmanned spacecraft have no one inside.

space probe An unmanned spacecraft sent to explore part of the solar system.

space shuttle A reusable spacecraft with wings. It carries astronauts between Earth and a space station. It also takes satellites into space and brings them back again.

sulfuric acid An oily liquid that can dissolve some substances.

terraforming Changing a planet so that it is more like Earth.

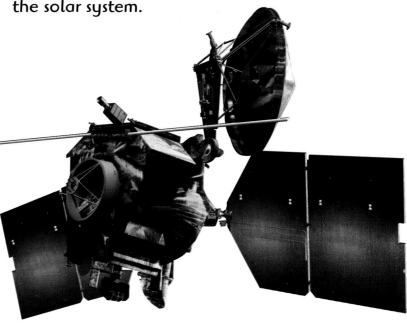

Index

WEB SITES

http://mars.jpl.nasa.gov/funzone_flash.html

http://dustbunny.com/afk/planets/mercury

http://kidsastronomy.com/venus.htm

http://www.esa.int/esaKIDSen/Earth.html

http://pds.jpl.nasa.gov/planets/

http://kids.nineplanets.org/